Companion Guide

Intimacy of the Best Kind
Is Truly Divine

Rachel L. Fox

Cover design by Pixel Studio
Edited by LACA Bridges
Author photo by George & Ciandra Pitts Photography

Scriptures quoted are from the King James Version, New King
James Version, and the Message Bible.

Printed in the United States of America by Basar Publishing

DEDICATION

I give all glory, honor and praise to my Lord and Savior Jesus Christ for giving me the strength and the inspiration to write this book. To my Mom Joyce C. Fox, thank you for walking upright before me - for teaching me what a true virtuous women is. For walking with the Lord and allowing me to see your one-on-one intimate relationship with God even after a divorce- thank you. You chose to live a single life before the Lord. I am eternally grateful for a mom like you; I wouldn't trade you for the world! This book is also dedicated to every single woman out there that has struggled in relationships or has had a hard time with your identity. I pray that this book will bless and change your life. It's time to be happily in love with Jesus, let's Start implementing and putting to action these words we have read!

TABLE OF CONTENTS

Letter from the Author……………….…....5
Dating Jesus…..6
1 On 1 with you Boo……………………..10
Love Letters to God…………...................15
Let God be your Man……………………..19
Falling in Love with Jesus…………….....25
Saying I Do…………………………....…..29
Sleeping with Jesus……………………….33
Released to Date Boaz……………..…….35
Definitions of Love………………….......39
About the Author……….............................43

Letter from the author

Hey friend!

I am excited you have this book in your hands it means that you are ready to start implementing and activating what you have been reading into your life. When I wrote Intimacy Of The Best Kind Is Truly Divine. I sought the father about how to help single women to learn the gift of singleness. Surprisingly he used a married man Mr. Damion bell to talk to me about the dating process and how to build a relationship with God the way I would dating a man. We talked about this almost 4 years ago and a light bulb went off. During this time Jesus began to take me through his process of dating him. One thing that God told me was that we all knew the dating process so well because we spend more time dating and getting to know other people then we do getting to know him. So he said this is how you will get others to develop a deep relationship with me in there singleness, by simply dating me. It seemed strange to me at first but I said ok Jesus It's a date! I say to you lady, it's time to date the most wonderful man ever. He will surpass anyone you have ever dated in the past. He is a true gentlemen and trust me he will never let you go. Dating Him will get you ready to date who he has for you. Jesus is Boaz number 1 and who he has for you is Boaz number 2. Are you ready? On your mark, get ready, get set, and go!!! Jesus is waiting on you!

Let's take off!
Rachel L. Fox

Smile Friend
Jesus loves
You boo!

Dating Jesus ~ Chapter 1

In this chapter we discussed a lot on getting to know the father through the dating process. Don't be afraid to move forward with dating Jesus he is the perfect gentlemen. Take a few moments and reflect and answer each question on the next page.

1. How does it feel to know that you can date Jesus?

_____

_____

_____

_____

_____

_____

_____

_____

_____

2. Now that you have started the process of dating Jesus, do you feel that you can live with or live without him? Explain your answer.

_____

_____

_____

_____

_____

_____

_____

_____

_____

_____

_____

_____

_____

_____

_____

_____

_____

_____

_____

_____

_____

3. Write down your first date with Jesus. Where did you go? How was your date? How did Jesus Make you feel? Was he a perfect gentlemen?

_____
_____
_____
_____
_____
_____
_____
_____
_____
_____
_____
_____
_____

4. How did you feel while out on a date with Jesus? Were you comfortable or did your first time feel a little different then a normal date would feel?

_____
_____
_____
_____
_____
_____
_____
_____
_____
_____
_____
_____
_____
_____
_____
_____
_____
_____

Notes

_____

_____

_____

_____

_____

_____

_____

_____

_____

_____

_____

_____

_____

_____

_____

_____

_____

_____

_____

_____

_____

_____

_____

_____

_____

_____

_____

_____

1-On-1 with you Boo ~Chapter 2

Now that you know that Jesus is you're boo! Began
to spend some one on one quality time with him. Answer
these questions after you have begun to spend a little time
with your new boo Jesus. He is the greatest Guy!

1. How did spending 1 on 1 Quality time with Jesus make you feel?

_____

_____

_____

_____

_____

_____

_____

_____

2. How do you think spending one on one time with Jesus made him feel?

_____

_____

_____

_____

_____

_____

_____

_____

_____

3. Ask Jesus about something simple like about what to eat or what to wear. What was his response to you?

_____

_____

_____

_____

_____

_____

_____

_____

_____

4. Try cooking with Jesus, What recipe and ingredients did he give? How was this experience and how did the food taste?

_____
_____
_____
_____
_____
_____
_____
_____
_____
_____
_____
_____
_____
_____
_____
_____
_____

5. How does it feel to know that Jesus can be your Boo?

_____
_____
_____
_____
_____
_____
_____
_____
_____
_____
_____
_____
_____
_____
_____
_____
_____

Notes

Notes

Love Letters to God ~ Chapter 3

God loves to hear what you think of him. Take a few minutes to write a love letter to God. It doesn't have to be a poem or in the style of the letters I wrote in my book Intimacy Of The Best Kind Is Truly Divine. Just write what's on your heart and mind.

1. My personal love Letter to God:

_____
_____
_____
_____
_____
_____
_____
_____
_____
_____
_____
_____
_____
_____
_____
_____
_____
_____
_____
_____
_____
_____

2. How did writing the love letter to God make you feel?

_____
_____
_____
_____
_____
_____
_____
_____
_____

3. How do you think your love letter made God feel?

_____
_____
_____
_____
_____
_____
_____
_____
_____
_____
_____
_____
_____
_____
_____
_____
_____
_____
_____
_____

4. Share with one of your single female friends and have them write a love letter to God and answer questions one and two.

Smile because God is sure smiling at you!

Notes

Let God Be Your Man ~ Chapter 4

Now that you have read about what it truly means to let God be your man, take some time and examine your life. Think about that time you spend with Jesus and the time you have spent with men. After doing this answer the questions on the following page.

1. Did you know that it is wrong to let an earthly man be your man before you allow God to be your man? How does this make you feel do you agree or disagree?

_____
_____
_____
_____
_____
_____
_____
_____
_____
_____
_____
_____
_____
_____
_____

2. Did you know that God is a jealous God and he desires to spend time with you? Did you know that God longs for a deep intimate relationship with you? How does knowing this make you feel?

_____
_____
_____
_____
_____
_____
_____
_____
_____
_____
_____
_____
_____

3. How do you think God feels when he can't spend time with you? Do you think he feels lonely or sad? How important do you think you are to God? Why do you feel the way you feel?

_____
_____
_____
_____
_____
_____
_____
_____
_____
_____
_____
_____
_____
_____

4. Have you given relationships with men more time then you have given Jesus? If so what was your reason? I had plenty of reasons, what pulled you away from Jesus?

_____
_____
_____
_____
_____
_____
_____
_____
_____
_____
_____
_____
_____
_____
_____

5. Did you know that given an earthly man more time then God is given that man the place of God? Which means that man is your God. Did you know that this angers God? Do you agree or disagree?

_____
_____
_____
_____
_____
_____
_____
_____
_____
_____
_____
_____
_____
_____
_____

6. Now that you know that God requires your time and wants to be your man before you date the man of God he has prepared for you. What will you do differently to make sure that you don't neglect Jesus?

_____
_____
_____
_____
_____
_____
_____
_____
_____
_____
_____

7. If you are that young woman like I was that gave more time to those men in relationships then you did to God read this prayer letter with me and get this in your heart mind and spirit. Remember Jesus loves you and only wants the best for you. Make sure to sign your name at the end of the prayer Letter as a declaration.

Father God in the name of Jesus,

I come to you right now with a repentant heart. Forgive me for putting earthly men before you. I apologize for neglecting you lord. I will make it my mission to please you and allow you into those deep dark intimate places in my life, before I ever share this with an earthly man. You are my God not these men I place you back in your rightful place as head of my life. Thank you for never leaving me lord even when I left you. I in return will try my hardest not to leave you again. I really need your help and Guidance to walk in complete oneness with you God. I recognize I was so wrong and I can't do things on my own. Thank you for being my man and for forgiving me. Thank you so much lord for loving me beyond my faults. You are the greatest man any woman could ever desire, and thank you for desiring a relationship with me. In Jesus name I pray amen.

With Love Your Godly Lady,

_____

Notes

Falling in Love with Jesus ~ Chapter 5

In this chapter we discussed what
It meant to fall in love with Jesus. This is very
important in this process of dating Jesus he
wants your heart and he wants you to have his
take some time and reflect and answer the
questions on the following page.

1. Falling In love With Jesus How does it feel to know that you can fall in love with Jesus?

_____

_____

_____

_____

_____

_____

_____

2. Did you know that God takes time for every person to get to know him this way? Write down the date that you have your love encounter with Jesus it is sure to change your life!

_____

_____

_____

_____

_____

_____

_____

_____

3. Falling in love with Jesus teaches us many
    Life changing things to help shape and mold us. Did you know that falling in love with Jesus teaches you how to love yourself completely?

_____

_____

_____

_____

_____

_____

_____

_____

_____

4. Did you know that loving Jesus prepares you to love your husband? Did you know that falling in love with Jesus prepares you for the love of the man of God that God has for you?

_____
_____
_____
_____
_____
_____
_____
_____
_____
_____
_____

5. As you go through this process of falling in love with Jesus write down life changing moments. What has falling in love with Jesus taught you?

_____
_____
_____
_____
_____
_____
_____
_____
_____
_____
_____
_____
_____
_____
_____

Notes

Saying I Do ~ Chapter 6

Saying I Do to Jesus is so rewarding. He will never let you down and he is always there for you even if you mess up along the way. Saying I Do to Jesus requires us to let go of our will and pick up his. Although tough, very rewarding and worth it. So ladies, please choose to say I Do today!

1. What is the one thing or things that God wants you to let go of
   in order to move forward in him? If you are unsure seek the
   father through fasting and prayer and he will reveal it to you.

_____

_____

_____

_____

_____

_____

_____

_____

_____

_____

_____

2. What was Gods command to you?

_____

_____

_____

_____

_____

_____

_____

_____

_____

_____

3. What was your response to God when he first showed you and
   told you what you needed to let go of?

_____

_____

_____

_____

_____

_____

_____

_____

_____

4. What was Gods response to your response to him about what he wanted you to let go of?

_____
_____
_____
_____
_____
_____
_____
_____
_____
_____
_____
_____
_____

5. Hurt and pain are part of the process. How did you feel while going through the process of letting go?

_____
_____
_____
_____
_____
_____
_____
_____
_____
_____

6. Remember that you must say I do to Jesus. What day, date, and time did you let go of you and your will and Say I Do to Jesus? This is your wedding date and future anniversary. Always remember the day you say I Do to Jesus.

_____
_____
_____
_____
_____
_____
_____

Notes

Sleeping With Jesus ~ Chapter 7

Learning to rest in the presence of the lord
Is so peaceful. You wake up a new person
the next morning it's simply amazing. Its time
to let God take control in our sleep when
we are unconcise. He will wrap you tight
and you will sleep great at night, but
don't take my word for
it just try him for yourself.

1. How does it feel to know that you can sleep with Jesus in a
   spiritual way?

_____

_____

_____

_____

_____

_____

_____

_____

_____

_____

2. Try sleeping with Jesus ask Him to wrap you in his presence
and just allow Him to comfort you and just drift off to sleep in God's
presence.

3. After falling asleep in God's presence, how did you wake up
the next morning feeling? Were you refreshed and renewed? Write
down your thoughts of this experience.

_____

_____

_____

_____

_____

_____

_____

_____

_____

_____

_____

_____

_____

_____

_____

_____

Released To Date Boaz ~ Chapter 8

In this chapter we talked about how Important it is to prepare yourself for your mate. Dating Jesus is what helps this process and really prepares you to date your future mate. Flip to the next page and answer these few questions and reflect on the information given in this book.

1. How does it feel to know that God trust you to date properly?

_____
_____
_____
_____
_____
_____
_____
_____
_____
_____
_____
_____
_____
_____
_____
_____

2. Write down your thoughts on what you are looking for in your ideal man of God.

_____
_____
_____
_____
_____
_____
_____
_____
_____
_____
_____
_____
_____
_____
_____

3. Have a talk with the lord about the type of man you want. What does he reveal to you? Write it down.

_____
_____
_____
_____
_____
_____
_____
_____
_____
_____
_____
_____
_____
_____
_____

4. Is the type of man that you desire, the man that God has for you? Does God have a different perspective? Trust me he knows best. What we want is not always what we need.

_____
_____
_____
_____
_____
_____
_____
_____
_____
_____
_____
_____
_____
_____
_____

Notes

_____

_____

_____

_____

_____

_____

_____

_____

_____

_____

_____

_____

_____

_____

_____

_____

_____

_____

_____

_____

_____

_____

_____

Definitions of Love ~ Chapter 9

Now that we have a greater understanding of the different types of love answer the following questions to distinguish the different types of love properly?

1. Which type of love do you feel is the appropriate type of love to love Jesus with?

_____

_____

_____

_____

_____

_____

_____

_____

_____

2. Which type of love does Jesus love us with?

_____

_____

_____

_____

_____

_____

_____

_____

_____

3. Which type of love is for a friendship or brotherly kind of love?

_____

_____

_____

_____

_____

_____

_____

_____

_____

4. Which type of love is for a family member?

_____
_____
_____
_____
_____
_____
_____
_____
_____
_____
_____
_____
_____
_____
_____
_____
_____

5. Which type of love should only be shared by married couples? Why?

_____
_____
_____
_____
_____
_____
_____
_____
_____
_____
_____
_____
_____
_____
_____
_____
_____
_____
_____

Notes

About the Author

Author Rachel Leanne Fox is a native of Newport News, Virginia. She was born on February 2, 1987 to Pastor Spencer L Fox Jr. (deceased) and Missionary Joyce C. Fox. She has one biological brother, Minister Daniel L. Fox and one half-brother, Mr. Brian L. Carter. She is a current student at Liberty University pursuing her degree in Early Childhood Education with a minor in Christian Counseling. She recently relocated to Maryland under the leading of Holy Spirit to pursue her God-ordained destiny as an author, anointed singer, songwriter, teacher and disciple of Jesus Christ. She is single, saved, and successful. Fox is also the owner of Torn II Perfection, a t-shirt and apparel design company. Additionally, she is the CEO of the T-Shirt Therapy Fashion Design Camps for youth. She is a member of The Way Clinic Ministries in Glen Burnie, Maryland under the leadership of Apostle Wayne Howden and Prophet Annie Howden. She is a member of T.E.N. Worldwide the Eagle Network and also a part of The Eagles International Author's Institute. Eagle-Author Rachel Leanne Fox is the author of *Intimacy Of The Best Kind Is Truly Divine* and *Intimacy Of The Best Kind Is Truly Divine the Companion Guide.* She is currently working on *Intimacy of the Best Kind is Truly Divine for Him,* the male version of the book as well as a cd of anointed songs and a series of children's books all to be released in the near future. This anointed woman-of-God has a heart for God and has a desire for his children to know just how much her God loves them.

Books written

ISBN: 978-1-942013-88-4

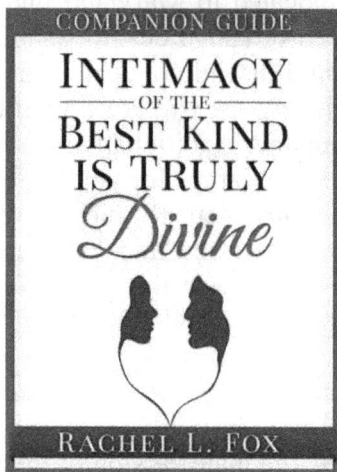

ISBN: 978-1-942013-89-1

www.ingramcontent.com/pod-product-compliance
Lightning Source LLC
Chambersburg PA
CBHW071748020426
42331CB00008B/2229